THE MATSUYAMA MIRROR

A full-length drama for young audiences by
Velina Hasu Houston

www.youthplays.com
info@youthplays.com
424-703-5315

COPYRIGHT RULES TO REMEMBER

CAST OF CHARACTERS

AIKO

TOORIKO

OKAASAN (also GRAND MISTRESS OF MATSUYAMA)

OTOOSAN

YUKIKO OBASAN

Aiko's Chorus of Dolls: FIRST KOKESHI

                                    SECOND KOKESHI

                                    THIRD KOKESHI

NOTE

One Kuro-ko (stage assistant in Japanese tradition) is needed. This responsibility can be carried out by any actor in the company.

SETTING

1600s. Matsuyama, Japan; and a magical world.

PROLOGUE

(Koto music plays. A Kuro-ko dances about setting props then assumes the waki position in the periphery.)

SCENE 1: THE GIFTS OF LIFE

(Lights fade up on Matsuyama, Japan. Early 1600s. Aiko and Tooriko's girlish bedroom. AIKO, her black hair in pigtails, sits on a futon folding origami. OKAASAN enters with a tray of tea, musubi, and fruit. Aiko bows her head toward her mother. Their love for one another apparent, they share the refreshment.)

AIKO: Will it be today, Okaasan?

OKAASAN: The horses tire easily in the snow. Otoosan did not expect snow. He never does well with the unexpected.

AIKO: I hope he brings me a pretty kokeshi doll.

OKAASAN: Kokeshi are for decoration. I make you soft dolls for play.

AIKO: But kokeshi are so colorful and beautiful.

OKAASAN: Aiko-chan, ne, everything you do flies in the face of tradition. Perhaps the time for dolls is over anyway.

AIKO: *(Surprised:)* Why?

OKAASAN: Father thinks you are too old for them.

AIKO: Oneesan maybe, but my dolls are my playmates.

OKAASAN: Your sister is your playmate.

AIKO: She is too old. She has forgotten how to play.

OKAASAN: I hope you never forget how to play.

AIKO: Forget? I shall never stop playing.

OKAASAN: One day all women must stop. But in your heart you must remember.

AIKO: ...what if one of us is different?

OKAASAN: And just who is that? Could it be Aiko the great child empress, protector of our rice fields and persimmon orchard?

AIKO: Yes! Aiko the adventuress! My dolls are my court! We will frolic, drink tea, and never live in anyone's shadow!

OKAASAN: And what about a husband, honorable adventuress?

AIKO: A husband interfering with tea and sweets? No-never-never-no!

OKAASAN: *(Amused:)* Oh, Aiko-chan, then the world would be turned upside down!

AIKO: Then I prefer a topsy-turvy world!

OKAASAN: *(A sigh us she playfully touches Aiko's braids:)* Dear Aiko-chan, it is hard to imagine you all grown up, married, with children of your own.

AIKO: No, never-never no.

OKAASAN: When you become a lady, Otoosan will take away your dolls and bring a handsome suitor who—

AIKO: When does it start, this questionable condition of being a lady?

OKAASAN: It starts in the body. *(Hesitant, pointing to her abdomen:)* Here.

AIKO: Like a stomachache?

OKAASAN: In a way, yes. Your body will...prepare itself for children.

AIKO: What? How?

OKAASAN: There is a...purification. And then you are a

woman.

AIKO: This sounds very serious, and yet it makes no sense at all.

OKAASAN: It is as if your body is...at war with itself. Although my sister always celebrates it.

AIKO: I hate war! War is for boys. How can Yukiko Obasan celebrate it? She is strange.

OKAASAN: Do you not one day wish to have children?

AIKO: Never-never no.

OKAASAN: You must have this stomach war if you want to have children.

AIKO: Who made such a contract? It seems quite unfair for girls and women!

OKAASAN: Well...

AIKO: Does Otoosan know the war is coming? Is that why he is so late returning home? He does not wish to see me change?

OKAASAN: He knows the time is coming when his last little girl changes forever. But it is the snow and— *(A pause.)* Shall I tell you a secret? These dolls of yours were mine once.

AIKO: But why did your father never take them away?

OKAASAN: They sat on the table looking beautiful. At night, I slipped them into my kimono and played with them in bed. When he caught me, I said I wanted to save them for the daughters I would someday have. But after you and Tooriko came I lost interest in dolls.

AIKO: How is that possible?

OKAASAN: *(A smile.)* It is a mystery.

AIKO: I never will.

OKAASAN: Time will tell. Your choices may change.

AIKO: No, never-never no. And I do not care if Father does not approve!

OKAASAN: He would curse the day that <u>my</u> father taught me to read and write!

AIKO: And then you taught me!

OKAASAN: I will always teach you, for I grew you inside of me like a flower. Come to me with every fear you have, no matter how small, ne, Aiko-chan?

AIKO: Can you stop the war from coming into my stomach?

OKAASAN: *(A gentle laugh, and then a pause.)* Your sister is contending with the war.

AIKO: She is like a samurai! She never cries out in pain!

OKAASAN: Maybe it is something that she welcomes, like my sister.

AIKO: If my sister were nicer, she would not have a stomach war.

OKAASAN: It comes once a month. It will be the same for you.

AIKO: That often?!

OKAASAN: Men say it keeps a woman honest.

AIKO: Then men should have war, too.

OKAASAN: They do. But a different kind.

AIKO: So will Tooriko make a baby now?

OKAASAN: Give her time, my child. She has only been married one season.

AIKO: Does she know how?

OKAASAN: *(Looking away to hide her amusement:)* Oh, I am certain she has learned by now.

(Enter TOORIKO with a basket of sewing. Her seriousness and formality are stark contrasts to Aiko's exuberance.)

TOORIKO: Good evening, Okaasan. Aiko, I heard you all the way down the corridor talking as loud as a boy. Let me tell you something, little sister, you have no choice but to grow up. And it could not happen soon enough for my tastes. You are completely uncivilized. Here.

(Hands her a sewing basket.)

Make yourself useful. Sew.

(Pinches Aiko.)

And never you mind about whether or not I shall have a baby! My husband is so busy cutting lumber in the mountains that I—

(Aiko ignores the offering of sewing.)

Sew and improve your domestic skills!

AIKO: No! And do not pinch me again or I will tell your husband about your bad gas!

TOORIKO: What did I tell you, Mother? Uncivilized as a monkey.

OKAASAN: You have gas?

AIKO: I do not wish to sew this evening! Otoosan will be home any moment and—

TOORIKO: Your embroidery work is less than perfect. Sew. When the childhood fat wears off your fingers, perhaps—

AIKO: My fingers are not fat! Yours are skinny like chopsticks. Chopstick-Fingers-Oneesan!

TOORIKO: *(Thrusting sewing basket at Aiko again:)* Here. Sew. Take it. Mother, make her take it. *(Sighs deeply.)* I thought I was rid of this waterbug when I married, but here I am waiting on this spoiled —

AIKO: Dear, sweet sister.

(Okaasan takes the sewing and hands it to Aiko who accepts it graciously, which irritates Tooriko.)

OKAASAN: Aiko-chan, let us embroider flowers.

TOORIKO: Embroider lilies. Be precise. Make it a present for Aunt Yukiko.

AIKO: I do not wish to sew for our grumpy old aunt.

OKAASAN: Aiko-chan! Do not speak that —

AIKO: She always unbraids my pigtails!

TOORIKO: Because they make you look like a little girl.

AIKO: I am a little girl!

TOORIKO: You must start behaving your —

AIKO: I will not act old like you.

TOORIKO: I am not old!

AIKO: You are cursed with stomach war, so —

TOORIKO: Be still and sew. You are too young to —

AIKO: But you just said that I am a lady!

TOORIKO: I take it back. You are a...an azuki bean!

AIKO: If I am a bean, then you are sea urchin!

OKAASAN: Aiko-chan, enough. Embroider.

TOORIKO: Yes. Embroider your lips together.

OKAASAN: Girls, please.

AIKO: Tell me, Oneesan, does it hurt when you have stomach—

TOORIKO: Ladies do not discuss such things.

AIKO: Then you are free to tell me!

TOORIKO: *(Wanting to terrify her:)* Yes! It hurts like 10 trampling horses, like high typhoon winds grinding through—

AIKO: Oh my goodness!

TOORIKO: *(Softening as she registers Aiko's terror:)* But when it starts, secrets unfold.

AIKO: What secrets?

OKAASAN: Do not tease Aiko-chan so, Tooriko-chan.

TOORIKO: Like playing games with your husband.

AIKO: Grown-up men play games with women?

TOORIKO: Oh yes.

OKAASAN: Tooriko!

TOORIKO: But you will never know, sitting here whining, suitors running away in hopes of more suitable—

OKAASAN: Tooriko, are you talking about the acquisition of a pet or a wife?

AIKO: Can Father stop the pain of trampling horses?

TOORIKO: *(Amused:)* Otoosan? He can do nothing in this matter but look the other way when the condition begins.

OKAASAN: In fact, your father will suddenly become speechless.

AIKO: But why? He is a strong man.

OKAASAN: Is it not true, Tooriko, that your father never knows what to say to you anymore?

TOORIKO: He found a nice husband for me. *(A pause, then:)* Be rebellious while you can, Aiko-chan. One day petals grow heavy.

AIKO: Petals?

OKAASAN: The worlds of love and marriage demand much of us, Aiko-chan.

AIKO: Are you happy, Okaasan?

OKAASAN: Sometimes in the morning when I wake up from dreams, I feel like my father's daughter. Then I look around me and realize that I am now my husband's wife and my children's mother. And that is fine because that is the natural order of things.

AIKO: What a somber business! No time for play! Tooriko-san, I will have to keep you from being a willow tree, weeping for eternity.

TOORIKO: I will not weep! I will stand erect like a pine. I will see over the mountains.

AIKO: Pining pine tree! Pining, pining pine tree!

TOORIKO: Oh the joys of having a little monkey sister!

AIKO: Thank you, big monkey sister!

OKAASAN: Girls, girls, please. Or should I say warriors. I hope your father brings you swords from his travels so that your battles can be fought to a proper and deserving finish. And then maybe, just maybe, there will be a moment of quiet—

AIKO: I hope he brings me a tall kokeshi with red lips and beautiful blackened teeth!

TOORIKO: I would like a lacquer comb with polished

abalone shell.

(Okaasan wanders to a window and stares outward into the night.)

AIKO: What would you like Father to bring you?

OKAASAN: *(Concerned:)* Just himself.

(Looks out of the window again.)

There is so much snow.

(Lights crossfade...)

SCENE 2: REFLECTIONS

(Several hours later. Low candlelight fades in on the bedroom. Aiko sleeps restlessly. Tooriko sits up anxiously. Aiko stirs.)

TOORIKO: Go back to sleep.

AIKO: Oneesan?

TOORIKO: What now?

AIKO: ...tell me about the stomach war.

TOORIKO: Fine, I will tell you since you will probably never get a chance to use its power on—

AIKO: Power?

TOORIKO: If you even hint you are having it, your husband will bring you sweets and have the maid cook your favorite foods.

AIKO: Truly?

TOORIKO: If you want time alone, hint again and he will leave thinking it is his escape but actually it is yours.

AIKO: Then I could play all night!

(Tooriko looks out of the window nervously, picks up her sewing, and starts to work on a piece of embroidery.)

Why must you sew at twilight?

TOORIKO: Because there is too much snow.

AIKO: Let it snow now that Father is home. Did he bring gifts? Did you see him before you fell asleep?

(Tooriko glances at her and then looks away quickly.)

TOORIKO: Here. Sew to keep your mind off our troubles.

AIKO: What troubles?

TOORIKO: Nothing. There are no troubles.

AIKO: Something is wrong. What is it? What is it? Tell me!

TOORIKO: Okaasan took the horse and rode into town to check on Father's travelling party...

AIKO: What? How long ago?

TOORIKO: Several hours.

AIKO: I shall go find her!

(Aiko tries to leave. Tooriko stops her.)

TOORIKO: A lady waits.

AIKO: I ride just as well as Father. Let me go!

TOORIKO: Not a man in Ehime prefecture will have you if you —

AIKO: I will wait for a man who will allow me to think!

TOORIKO: Then you will be waiting for a long time.

(Sounds of horses are heard from off stage. Aiko tries to run out, but is stopped by OTOOSAN who enters covered with snow. He conceals grimness with a smile for his children. He carries a satchel filled to capacity.)

OTOOSAN: Good daughters. Hello.

TOORIKO: *(Bowing low:)* Welcome home, Otoosan.

AIKO: Welcome, Father.

OTOOSAN: Where are you going in such a hurry, Aiko?

TOORIKO: Out into the snow to find you!

AIKO: Where is Mother?

OTOOSAN: It is so cold. Let me sit for a —

AIKO: Is she with the horses?

TOORIKO: Quiet, Aiko!

(Tooriko helps him off with his coat. He and Tooriko sit around the candle. Incredulous, Aiko puts on her father's coat and prepares to leave.)

OTOOSAN: Take off my coat and sit, Aiko.

AIKO: Tell me where she is.

OTOOSAN: <u>Sit</u>.

(Otoosan takes the coat off of her and forces her to sit.)

Children, your mother has...left us.

AIKO: What? No. <u>No</u>.

OTOOSAN: ...there has been...an accident.

(The breath knocked out of her, Aiko sits motionlessly. Tooriko is quiet with shock for a moment and then weeps uncontrollably.)

AIKO: *(Eerie calmness:)* You must tell me what has happened to my mother.

OTOOSAN: The snow. An accident with the horses. Her head struck a rock. When they found her, she was already...

AIKO: How can you sit there like a piece of stone?

TOORIKO: Aiko!

AIKO: How can you? What are you?

OTOOSAN: The bearer of our pain so that you can go on.

TOORIKO: Oh, this family. Pull yourself together, Father.

OTOOSAN: Your mother drifts in the winds tonight, seeking her next existence. We must keep the sky clear; we must not weep.

AIKO: Bring her back. *(To the ether:)* Come back, Okaasan. Come back! Please, please, come back.

OTOOSAN: Enough, gentle Aiko-chan...we must go on as usual...

AIKO: What? How?

TOORIKO: Shall we sit around like fools and weep?

AIKO: You never loved her like I did.

TOORIKO: I am older and I have loved her longer.

AIKO: And I love her best.

(Otoosan reaches for the satchel and removes two packages.)

OTOOSAN: Here. Your gifts. Come. Let us be as curious and happy as we always are when I return from my journeys.

AIKO: I want only the return of my mother.

OTOOSAN: What do you think I brought you, Aiko-chan?

AIKO: Who will I ask for help when I am learning new embroidery?

TOORIKO: I will help you.

AIKO: You do not help. You order.

OTOOSAN: We will all help each other.

AIKO: Tooriko-san will only help herself and her husband.

TOORIKO: What is wrong with that? If you ever grow up, you will bring a husband to live here with you and Otoosan.

You will know secrets that will make you selfish sometimes, too.

OTOOSAN: Yes, Aiko. I will find you a strong, patient man.

TOORIKO: In this case, perhaps a saint is required.

OTOOSAN: And Tooriko will always be near. Her husband plans to build their new house just on the other side of the village.

AIKO: It might as well be on the other side of the universe.

OTOOSAN: When I am gone, you two sisters will be all that is left of our family. Can you not be civil to one another? Come, Aiko-chan. Come sit by me.

AIKO: Who will cook tonight, Otoosan?

TOORIKO: I will cook.

AIKO: You? The taste will kill— Sorry. But you don't know how to cook. You don't.

OTOOSAN: Your aunt will come tomorrow to help.

AIKO: Aunt Yukiko!

OTOOSAN: This is a time to find strength in family. Yukiko Obasan is good and kind.

AIKO: And rough as a tree trunk.

TOORIKO: But sturdy and lasting.

OTOOSAN: Are you not curious about your present, Aiko? Perhaps it will give you a little light in this darkness?

AIKO: *(Facetiously:)* Oh I am certain.

OTOOSAN: Then if I have brought a new doll, must I find another little girl to give it to?

AIKO: Otoosan? Could the gods have made a mistake? Can they be persuaded to give back my mother?

OTOOSAN: Open your present, dear child.

AIKO: How can I behold these gifts at such a time?

TOORIKO: Because we need to. If I stare at the tatami all night and cry, then I will not make it to morning.

OTOOSAN: Here, Tooriko-san.

(She opens her gift. It is a scarf.)

TOORIKO: Thank you, Otoosan. I shall save it.

OTOOSAN: Do not save it. Wear it. Make yourself look beautiful. Today. Now. And for you, Aiko-chan.

(He takes out a silver, sparkling box. Immediately, the Kuro-ko tinkles wind chimes and Aiko looks around, startled as if she hears something. Aiko holds the box and slowly opens it, scattering sparkling dust. She takes out a large silver and gold lacquered mirror with angel hair hanging in shreds from it. It leaves her in a state of awe. Tooriko is afraid of it.)

AIKO: What is it, Father?

OTOOSAN: It is called a "mirror."

AIKO: "...mirror..."

TOORIKO: Does it belong in the house?

OTOOSAN: It is magic. Look in the glass.

AIKO: *(Startled:)* There is a girl in the glass!

OTOOSAN: *(Laughs.)* And who does she look like?

(Aiko dares look again and gasps. Tooriko's curiosity is quelled by fear.)

AIKO: It is Mother, when she was a young girl!

(Tooriko screams in fright and Otoosan silences her with a gentle look.)

OTOOSAN: It seems so, does it not?

AIKO: Mother has become a child in this mirror. How can that be so? What have you done? Have you put her in the mirror? Can I get her out?

TOORIKO: No! No! We will all be cursed.

OTOOSAN: Whenever you miss your mother, look in this mirror and you will find her looking back at you.

(Warm, loving woman's laughter is heard only by Aiko who jumps in surprise and fear.)

TOORIKO: *(Staring at her:)* You are possessed.

AIKO: There is a spirit in the mirror! I can hear her; can you hear—

OTOOSAN: No one else in Matsuyama has such a mirror. You will be the talk of the town.

TOORIKO: And not just because of this mirror.

(Aiko brandishes the mirror toward her sister who jumps in fright.)

Keep that thing away from me! It is black magic.

OTOOSAN: It is healing magic.

(Removes a porcelain doll from his satchel.)

I brought this porcelain doll for your mother.

(He offers it to Tooriko, but she motions for him to offer it to Aiko. He hands it to Aiko. Her pleasure gives Tooriko pleasure.)

For you, Aiko-chan.

AIKO: Thank you, Otoosan.

(He picks up his things and leaves. Tooriko tries to blow out the candle and Aiko stops her.)

Leave it be.

TOORIKO: But it is almost burned away. There is no use for it.

AIKO: Let it burn and, when it is gone, I want its scent to linger in my hair and kimono.

TOORIKO: Little sister, learn to be practical. As you can see, our parents are not immortal.

AIKO: But they are. Mother lives. I saw her in this mirror.

TOORIKO: Put that thing away!

AIKO: But I really saw her. I did!

TOORIKO: Aiko-chan, childhood is a butterfly feeding on the dew of youth. And the dew disappears quickly. You <u>must</u> grow up.

AIKO: No. Never-never-no.

TOORIKO: Oh, how can you behave so when she has died this night? Do you not see that the gods have punished her for riding out into the snow like a soldier?

AIKO: She <u>is</u> a soldier, a soldier of the soul, like me! I shall ride, too, and I will return in one piece with Mother at my side.

TOORIKO: Dear Aiko... Good night.

AIKO: The night shall never be good again.

(Tooriko leaves. Aiko stares into the mirror as the Kuro-ko tinkles the wind chimes. Lights crossfade...)

SCENE 3: TREE TRUNKS

(Lights fade in on the bedroom. YUKIKO OBASAN cleans the room with obsessive efficiency. As she dusts, she sees Aiko's kokeshi dolls and sighs in disgust. Aiko tiptoes into the room and

Yukiko Obasan whirls around with a sixth sense.)

YUKIKO OBASAN: Why were you sneaking in here?

AIKO: I did not wish to disturb you, Obasan.

YUKIKO OBASAN: Come here. Now.

AIKO: No thank you.

YUKIKO OBASAN: How my sister let you run around in these pigtails at your age is beyond me.

(Yukiko Obasan tries to unbraid Aiko's pigtails as Aiko fidgets.)

AIKO: Stop it! Please!

YUKIKO OBASAN: Stop wiggling like a snake.

AIKO: *(Leaping from her aunt's arms:)* Are you so familiar with snakes?

YUKIKO OBASAN: It is time to be rid of your dolls as well.

AIKO: You cannot take away my toys!

YUKIKO OBASAN: Now that I am running this household for your father, it is time you acted your —

AIKO: You sleep in my mother's bed!

YUKIKO OBASAN: Where else am I to sleep? In the stables with the horses?

AIKO: I am certain that could be arranged.

YUKIKO OBASAN: As custom has it, when a mother dies, her sister comes to help.

AIKO: By marrying your sister's husband?

YUKIKO OBASAN: Look at you, so unlady-like. Come here and sit down so that I may loosen your hair from —

AIKO: My mother will come back and you will be chased out in the middle of the night!

YUKIKO OBASAN: And will you stay here all alone when your father must travel to market? How will a mere child fend —

AIKO: I am an adventuress.

YUKIKO OBASAN: Is that so? What if goblins and ogres come?

AIKO: I will think them to death! *(A beat.)* Besides, I am never alone, not with my mother and my mirror.

YUKIKO OBASAN: Your what? "Mirror"? Are you speaking of magic?

AIKO: Yes! I know magic!

YUKIKO OBASAN: Show it to me.

AIKO: It is a special gift from my father so —

YUKIKO OBASAN: It is all right. You can show it to me.

(Aiko does not respond.)

Aiko-chan...I am your...new mother.

AIKO: No thank you.

YUKIKO OBASAN: I will cook and help you with your sewing. And, like my sister, I can read and write. I will help you with —

AIKO: No thank you.

YUKIKO OBASAN: Be still.

AIKO: No!

(Aiko tries to leave the room and her aunt stops her.)

YUKIKO OBASAN: I said sit! I will teach you civility if it is the last thing I —

AIKO: No! Never-never no!

YUKIKO OBASAN: Stop talking nonsense!

(Aiko fights, tears falling, and Yukiko Obasan forces her to sit while she undoes her ponytail. Aiko cries.)

AIKO: You smell like onions.

YUKIKO OBASAN: Thank you, dear child.

AIKO: Like soggy squid that has sat in the sun for days.

YUKIKO OBASAN: Bless you, sweet princess.

AIKO: I also detect a strong odor of wild animal feces.

YUKIKO OBASAN: All beings have waste. Some of us learn not to waste and —

AIKO: What? You do not —?

YUKIKO OBASAN: You are just as ridiculous as my sis —

AIKO: Stop. Just go. Go home.

YUKIKO OBASAN: This is my home now.

AIKO: This is my mother's home.

YUKIKO OBASAN: ...it was... *(A pause.)* ...may I prepare something special for you? Is there something that you would like?

AIKO: *(A pause then:)* Yes.

YUKIKO OBASAN: Wonderful. What would you like?

AIKO: Mongolian bamboo shoots.

YUKIKO OBASAN: I would have to go to Mongolia for that.

AIKO: *(With malevolent delight:)* Yes.

(Yukiko Obasan finishes unbraiding her ponytail.)

YUKIKO OBASAN: There. Now see how beautiful you look. The young men of Matsuyama will stand in line to have the hand of a lady like you.

(Yukiko Obasan opens Aiko's mouth and examines her teeth.)

And you have perfect teeth as well.

AIKO: That is what father says when he buys a new horse.

(Yukiko Obasan tries to manage the strain as she puts the kokeshi dolls into a furoshiki and ties it up.)

YUKIKO OBASAN: Now I want you to show me that you are willing to cooperate. Take these dolls to the attic.

(Aiko opens the furoshiki and studies her dolls with love.)

They are just things. Little girl things.

(Aiko slips her mirror out of her kimono sleeve and stares into it as wind chimes tinkle. Startled, Yukiko Obasan looks around.)

Did you just hear something?

(Aiko puts the mirror away.)

AIKO: Okaasan says I may keep my dolls.

YUKIKO OBASAN: What is that you are hiding in your sleeve? Let me see it.

AIKO: I think not.

YUKIKO OBASAN: Is it that magic? Your "mirror"?

AIKO: Careful where you go today! Something could —

(At her wit's end, Yukiko Obasan returns the dolls to the furoshiki.)

YUKIKO OBASAN: If you do not put these away, I will use them in the cooking fire tonight!

AIKO: I hate you! You are a thief!

(Aiko takes the package and leaves angrily. Yukiko Obasan feels tormented and inept. Lights crossfade.)

SCENE 4: HUMAN BEINGS ARE NOT
DESIGNED VERY WELL

(Lights fade up on an open road. Aiko wears a scarf and jacket. She carries two furoshiki. She sits looking from right to left. Tooriko appears also dressed warmly.)

TOORIKO: What are you doing on the outer roadway?

AIKO: I am going to town.

TOORIKO: By yourself? Come back to the house this instant.

AIKO: I am a young lady, am I not? I may travel the world alone.

TOORIKO: Silly Aiko-chan. You will get a chill.

AIKO: Yukiko Obasan is pretending to be our mother.

TOORIKO: She is only trying to help. You are too young to be without a —

AIKO: I am terribly old.

TOORIKO: Do you require a cane?

AIKO: Do not tell Father that I am on the roadway.

TOORIKO: What have you there in your furoshiki?

AIKO: My dolls.

TOORIKO: You run away with your dolls and not food to eat?

AIKO: I am not running away!

TOORIKO: Even so, the road to town is a long one. Dolls will not keep you warm.

AIKO: Yukiko Obasan was going to burn them in the fire.

TOORIKO: You are exaggerating. Come back to the house with me. I will protect your dolls.

AIKO: Why?

TOORIKO: Because I must. Come, little bean of mine.

AIKO: Maybe she will even burn me in the fire if she thinks I am no longer of any good use.

TOORIKO: Little sister. I understand. Perhaps we should hide the dolls in a special place.

AIKO: She would find them. She has explored every nook and cranny of our home in just a few days. She wants to do the same with me, clean me, dust me off, and try to make me hers.

TOORIKO: Come. Together we will find a place for your dolls.

AIKO: You would defy her for me?

TOORIKO: Today I will.

AIKO: Why today?

TOORIKO: Because my husband will come for me in the morning and I will go to my home.

AIKO: But our home is your home.

TOORIKO: Not anymore. I must make a new one.

AIKO: Why?

TOORIKO: Come, little sister. Let us carry out our family task and save your dolls for your daughters.

AIKO: Daughters! Never-never-no. I will have sons, so they need never worry about being good ladies.

TOORIKO: But sons must worry about being men.

AIKO: Human beings are not designed very well.

TOORIKO: It all works out. You will see. Come.

AIKO: You go back to the house. I will come shortly. I want to see if it will snow.

TOORIKO: It has not snowed since our mother passed.

AIKO: Since she <u>went</u> <u>away</u>. *(A pause.)* The snow will come again.

TOORIKO: Very well. I cannot stand the cold.

AIKO: It is warm. Bury your feet in the snow and it feels like a blanket.

TOORIKO: *(A smile.)* Dreamer child.

(Tooriko exits, patting Aiko on the head. Aiko cries. She unwraps her dolls and kisses them. She takes out her mirror and stares at it.)

AIKO: Mother? Where are you? Can you hear me? How am I to live without you?

(She musters a smile for the reflection as wind chimes tinkle and the woman's laughter is heard. Aiko looks around trying to find the voice. She puts everything away and runs about in a hurry.)

Mother? Okaasan? Is that you? It is you, yes?

(Aiko stumbles and falls. The Kuro-ko goes to her side and holds her. Lights crossfade...)

SCENE 5: SUGAR AND SPICE AND EVERYTHING NICE

(Lights fade up on a scrim that represents Aiko's lacquered mirror. Images of Aiko appear on the scrim. Aiko is on the ground and being held by the Kuro-ko. She looks up and stares at the scrim "mirror." She tries to run toward it but cannot, as if there is an invisible force in her way. Wind chimes tinkle and the laughter is heard again.)

AIKO: Okaasan? I know it is you! I knew you would not abandon your promises. Okaasan!

(Aiko tries to approach the scrim again, but this time is yanked

back by the invisible force. She begins to dance as if being pulled by this force. Kuro-ko and Tooriko, in a kokeshi mask, join Aiko in her dance. Classic shakuhachi music fades in. She falls beside the mirror and is surrounded by red chiffon scarves [these can be pulled from the handle of the mirror]. The stream of scarves is endless and overwhelms her. The invisible force pulls her in frenzy as she begins to dance again. The scarves are a part of a red chiffon kimono that she dons during the dance. The scarves trail and billow. The dance comes to a pitch and Aiko collapses on the floor. The music ceases. Aiko whimpers and moans. She is so exhausted that she cannot lift her head. Then the wind chimes begin to tinkle again. Exit Tooriko. The Kuro-ko pushes Aiko toward the scrim and resumes the waki position. The scrim is backlit and the images of Aiko disappear. Behind the scrim appear three giggling and shuffling figures like children at play. They are representations of kokeshi with masks that reflect the wooden texture and painted markings of traditional kokeshi. Their simple kimono are in the same style as their masks. They have butterfly wings on their backs. They are innocent and curious. Their tone is staccato, rhythmic. They speak rapidly in high register, with upward inflection. They stare at Aiko's figure through the scrim.)

KOKESHI: What is it?

FIRST KOKESHI: It is a doll.

SECOND & THIRD KOKESHI: What a beautiful doll! Let us invite it to play with us!

(Through a split in the scrim, the Kokeshi hesitantly approach Aiko. They touch and sniff her. One pulls a long chain of lilies out of her kimono sleeve and tickles Aiko's nose with it. One pokes at her.)

SECOND KOKESHI: Hello, little doll!

AIKO: *(Weakly:)* Have you seen my mother?

(The Kokeshi jump and gasp.)

THIRD KOKESHI: It speaks! Why it is not a doll at all!

FIRST KOKESHI: It certainly is not one of us!

(Touches Aiko's forehead.)

Ooh! She feels soft like warm o-mochi!

THIRD KOKESHI: *(Using a special power to make this discovery:)* It...is a little girl!

SECOND KOKESHI: How lovely! We need a little girl to play with!

FIRST KOKESHI: I do not remember girls!

THIRD KOKESHI: Remember soft and sweet, pink hearts, ticklish feet?

SECOND KOKESHI: Remember from the fairy tales, the little girls with far to go?

FIRST KOKESHI: Oh yes! I remember!

(The Second and Third Kokeshi try to take Aiko into their world.)

But wait! I think she is hurt!

KOKESHI: We will have to take her home with us. We will have to make her our own.

THIRD KOKESHI: What is your name, little girl?

(The Kokeshi surround Aiko with the chain of lilies. They hold her like a baby, and fan and caress her.)

(As if in a trance with her special powers:) She is Aiko. She wants to be here with us.

SECOND KOKESHI: But she asked for "mother." What is "mother"?

THIRD KOKESHI: We will ask the Grand Mistress of Matsuyama.

SECOND KOKESHI: Oh no. We must play first!

FIRST KOKESHI: She cannot play. She is hurt.

(They all sniff her again.)

THIRD KOKESHI: But we can make her well.

FIRST KOKESHI: But she is not a kokeshi doll. Maybe she is not meant to enter the mirror.

SECOND KOKESHI: You always want to make the rules for our play. I say we should take her home.

THIRD KOKESHI: I have never had a girl toy before.

(Aiko sneezes and the Kokeshi run for the scrim. They stand just inside and stare at her. She struggles to raise her head and sees them.)

AIKO: Please help me.

KOKESHI: Are you going to blow up?

AIKO: I simply sneezed.

KOKESHI: Sneezed! *(They giggle.)* We do not know "sneeze."

(Aiko sneezes again, causing them to ooh, aah, and titter with enthusiasm.)

You are a good girl toy!

AIKO: I need to find my mother. Have you seen—

KOKESHI: What is "mother"?

AIKO: *(Startled:)* Wait a minute. I know you.

KOKESHI: Oh no, never-never-no.

AIKO: Yes! You are my dolls!

KOKESHI: *(Laughter.)* We do not belong to you! We belong to spring!

AIKO: *(Confused:)* Do you not remember? I saved you from my wicked aunt Yukiko just yesterday.

FIRST KOKESHI: What is "yesterday"?

AIKO: The day before today.

SECOND KOKESHI: What is "today"?

AIKO: It is time.

THIRD KOKESHI: What is time?

AIKO: Minutes and hours that tell you when to eat, sleep, when to stop playing —

FIRST KOKESHI: Stop playing?!

KOKESHI: What?!

FIRST KOKESHI: How absurd!

SECOND KOKESHI: Utterly boring!

THIRD KOKESHI: There is no time here, thank goodness!

KOKESHI: Let us play! You are one of us now!

(The Kokeshi giggle like human wind chimes. Aiko begins crawling to the scrim. Finally, she reaches it. The Kokeshi look at one another and finally decide to drag her in. The minute she enters their world, Aiko is renewed. The Kokeshi are delighted. They remove her red kimono and cast it outside the scrim. The Japanese children's song, "Haru Ga Kita," fades in [an instrumental version]. They begin playing with great delight, using the lily chain as a toy. They dance and skip. Outside the scrim, Otoosan enters and sees the red kimono. It startles him. He picks up the mirror and looks around in panic.)

OTOOSAN: Aiko-chan? Aiko!

(He runs out. Aiko suddenly looks in his direction. She goes to

the edge of the scrim and the Kokeshi pull her back.)

KOKESHI: Where are you going? Do not leave us.

AIKO: It is time for dinner. I must put you away and go home.

KOKESHI: We need never be put away again. We play forever!

AIKO: But surely you must stop to eat and sleep?

KOKESHI: Oh no. We are never hungry.

AIKO: But you must have reading and writing lessons with your tutor.

KOKESHI: Oh no. Never-never-no.

AIKO: What about your sewing? Are your stitches perfect?

KOKESHI: Perfect life! No curse! Never nervous!

AIKO: But sometimes you have to follow rules, do you not?

KOKESHI: We know everything that a doll must know to be happy. Do you know everything that a little girl must know to be happy?

AIKO: *(Sadly:)* No.

KOKESHI: Then you need a teacher!

FIRST KOKESHI: Perhaps the Grand Mistress of Matsuyama?

(At the mention of this name, all of the Kokeshi bow low with reverence and then rise up again giggling.)

SECOND KOKESHI: Oh, but we are having so much fun at play. Can it not wait?

AIKO: I want to find my mother. I have something very important to tell her.

SECOND KOKESHI: What could be more important than playing?

AIKO: Something is happening to me that only my mother can explain.

THIRD KOKESHI: Remember, she is from a different world! Things happen to little girls!

FIRST and SECOND KOKESHI: Oh dear! Oh dear-oh dear-oh dear!

FIRST KOKESHI: Are you dying? In fairy tales, human beings die.

SECOND KOKESHI: Are you lost in the woods?

THIRD KOKESHI: Did you eat a bad apple?

FIRST KOKESHI: No-no-no. Wait. Let us just ask it.

SECOND KOKESHI: Yes, it truly cannot be avoided!

THIRD KOKESHI: Did you...did you tell a lie?

KOKESHI: Lying is bad! Very, very bad!

AIKO: I have run away from home.

FIRST KOKESHI: Run away! Why that is terrible too!

KOKESHI: But why? Why oh why?

AIKO: Because my aunt has stolen my father.

KOKESHI: Ummm. Stealing is very bad.

AIKO: She loves him and —

KOKESHI: Oh! Love is very, very good!

AIKO: But the worst of it is I have been cursed.

(The Kokeshi gasp in unison.)

FIRST KOKESHI: Is it catching?

AIKO: No. You are dolls. You are safe from this condition.

SECOND KOKESHI: Condition?

AIKO: Of course, some say it is power.

FIRST KOKESHI: Like magic?!

AIKO: I am not certain, but something tells me that I do not want it in my life.

SECOND KOKESHI: Why not?

AIKO: Because it will make me have a stomachache.

SECOND KOKESHI: You need pickled plum tea! Bye-bye tummy-ache!

THIRD KOKESHI: No, no. I know what it is.

FIRST & SECOND KOKESHI: What is it? What is it?

THIRD KOKESHI: It is the most interesting thing about little girls.

SECOND KOKESHI: Uh-oh! What have you done?

AIKO: I have done nothing wrong!

THIRD KOKESHI: It is not something that you do. It just happens.

FIRST KOKESHI: What is it? Does she have an illness?

THIRD KOKESHI: Little girls...grow up.

AIKO: I am afraid that is what is happening to me.

KOKESHI: We are sorry! So very sorry!

(*Aiko points outside of the scrim to the red kimono.*)

AIKO: I have a stomach war inside.

SECOND KOKESHI: A stomach war? How awful sounding! Is it worse than a stomachache?

AIKO: Your insides grumble and —

FIRST KOKESHI: Oh dear! Must not grumble! Must not mumble! Must —

AIKO: It is very serious! You change!

FIRST & SECOND KOKESHI: Oh my.

FIRST KOKESHI: It sounds like death!

AIKO: It is meant to be a sign of life.

THIRD KOKESHI: Oh! That is power! Power is good!

SECOND KOKESHI: But you are okay now, are you not?

AIKO: *(Startled:)* That is true! The pain has stopped.

FIRST KOKESHI: Yes! So you must stay. You are safe here.

SECOND KOKESHI: No pain! All gain!

THIRD KOKESHI: No typhoons! No monsoons!

FIRST KOKESHI: Just play, play, play! Nothing will stop you from playing!

THIRD KOKESHI: We will take you to see the Grand Mistress of Matsuyama.

AIKO: The way you say her name, she must be very grand!

KOKESHI: No one grander!

AIKO: Is she...imposing?

(The Kokeshi look at one another, perplexed.)

You know...is she...formidable? Most people in charge of things are. My father is —

FIRST KOKESHI: Oh no-no-no! She is gentle!

SECOND KOKESHI: She is majestic!

THIRD KOKESHI: She is one of the nicest I have ever met.

She is a woman.

AIKO: Why would she want to help me?

FIRST KOKESHI: She knows all about The Other Side!

AIKO: Can she help me find my mother? I think she is here! I heard her laughter.

KOKESHI: Come! Come-come-come!

(The Kokeshi giggle and pull Aiko in different directions as "Haru Ga Kita" fades up again instrumentally. Upstage, from behind the scrim, a figure in a long, exaggerated kimono decorated with lilies appears. She wears a crown of lilies. It is the spirit of THE GRAND MISTRESS OF MATSUYAMA. She walks formally. She encircles the group and they stop playing. The Kokeshi fall to their knees in bows. Aiko is in awe and then recognition sets in.)

AIKO: Okaasan?

KOKESHI: Honorable Respectable Sincere Loving Sensitive Creative Kind Beautiful Grand Mistress of Matsuyama!

AIKO: No, this is my mother.

KOKESHI: Shhhh!

AIKO: And you are my dolls.

KOKESHI: Quiet!

AIKO: I fell in the snow and I looked in the mirror and... *(To The Grand Mistress of Matsuyama:)* Are you my mother?

THE GRAND MISTRESS OF MATSUYAMA: I am all mothers.

AIKO: Will you be mine today?

THE GRAND MISTRESS OF MATSUYAMA: Are you a flower?

AIKO: Yes.

THE GRAND MISTRESS OF MATSUYAMA: Then I know I can help you because I am also a flower.

KOKESHI: Tulips! Daisies! Chrysanthemums! Lilies! Hydrangea, hydrangea, hydrangea! Ajisai— — — — — — *(This with a long sigh.)*

AIKO: Mother, I—

THE GRAND MISTRESS OF MATSUYAMA: Yes.

AIKO: I have started having stomach wars.

THE GRAND MISTRESS OF MATSUYAMA: Ah...

KOKESHI: Poor little girl. If only she were a doll!

THE GRAND MISTRESS OF MATSUYAMA: Oh no. We must offer congratulations.

AIKO: Congratulations?

THE GRAND MISTRESS OF MATSUYAMA: Yes. You are becoming powerful.

KOKESHI: Ohhhh!

THE GRAND MISTRESS OF MATSUYAMA: Can you not feel it?

AIKO: *(Confused:)* No.

THE GRAND MISTRESS OF MATSUYAMA: Aiko-chan—

AIKO: But how do you know my name if you are not—

THE GRAND MISTRESS OF MATSUYAMA: It is dinnertime and you are here playing, forever playing. Is that what you desire?

AIKO: Father has married Yukiko Obasan and she sleeps in your bed and snoops all over the house.

THE GRAND MISTRESS OF MATSUYAMA: Your father needs a wife and you need a mother.

(Aiko wants to reach out to The Grand Mistress of Matsuyama, but cannot touch her, as if there is an invisible wall between them. They reach their fingertips toward one another.)

AIKO: I intended to go home for dinner, but my dolls want to play and play.

KOKESHI: Jump and roll and skip and leap! Oh yes! Always-always-yes!

THE GRAND MISTRESS OF MATSUYAMA: You must make a decision, Aiko-chan.

AIKO: I came looking for you because of the curse of stomach wars.

THE GRAND MISTRESS OF MATSUYAMA: But it endows us as well, with richness, fruitfulness, boys and girls.

KOKESHI: Make us one little, two little, three little girls! All for here! Nothing to fear!

THE GRAND MISTRESS OF MATSUYAMA: In our world there is no pain, only light.

KOKESHI: Sunbeams, moonbeams, starry bright!

AIKO: But you said, I mean my mother said, it was unlikely that I could avoid the stomach wars.

THE GRAND MISTRESS OF MATSUYAMA: Here, yes. Just like the dolls. But dolls cannot grow up. You may stay here and roll in the clouds all your life long. You need never look into a human face again. You can play forever and never know any pain, any heartache.

AIKO: But I am not a doll!

THE GRAND MISTRESS OF MATSUYAMA: Are you

certain?

KOKESHI: She smells like a girl!

AIKO: These are the dolls. My silly kokeshi.

THE GRAND MISTRESS OF MATSUYAMA: Then, dear one, shall you return home for dinner and sit at the table as an adult with your father and aunt...your new mother?

AIKO: New mother? I only have <u>one</u> mother.

THE GRAND MISTRESS OF MATSUYAMA: Never turn away from love, any love.

AIKO: If it is real!

THE GRAND MISTRESS OF MATSUYAMA: Shall you go home now?

KOKESHI: Only our love is real? Oh no, do not go! Stay here, always-always-yes!

THE GRAND MISTRESS OF MATSUYAMA: Do you choose to be a doll and play forever?

KOKESHI: Oh yes! Come, Aiko the adventuress! Aiko the adventuress!

AIKO: But I do not like my aunt.

THE GRAND MISTRESS OF MATSUYAMA: She is not the only thing you must accept. Your father is different now, trying to find his way in a world that excludes your mother. Your sister also struggles with the unevenness of a new life as a wife.

AIKO: You mean she is not happy?

THE GRAND MISTRESS OF MATSUYAMA: Some days are pink and others grey. *(A pause.)* Then there are all the rules.

KOKESHI: Despicable, despicable, DESPICABLE! Rules-fools-

fools-rules-yucky-unlucky-never-never —

THE GRAND MISTRESS OF MATSUYAMA: Kokeshi, onegai shimasu! You will scare her away.

AIKO: My head was spinning!

THE GRAND MISTRESS OF MATSUYAMA: Yes. Without order life is like an unkept house.

AIKO: But Yukiko Obasan wants to take away my dolls and make me wear my hair "like a lady"!

(The Kokeshi begin to giggle and tug at Aiko.)

FIRST KOKESHI: Like a lady!

SECOND KOKESHI: Ooh-ooh-ooh!

AIKO: Please tell them to stop playing.

THE GRAND MISTRESS OF MATSUYAMA: But that is what they are created to do. What of you, my young lady? What is it that you are meant to be and do?

KOKESHI: Come play with us, little girl!

AIKO: Stop it, you silly dolls.

KOKESHI: Silly is good! Silly, willy, shrilly, frilly!

THE GRAND MISTRESS OF MATSUYAMA: Say the word and I shall close the doors to that other world.

(Aiko looks toward the opening of the scrim. Outside the scrim, the Kuro-ko scatters crimson petals around the stage and dances with the red chiffon scarved kimono, beckoning her.)

AIKO: But if I go back, will you come with me, Okaasan?

THE GRAND MISTRESS OF MATSUYAMA: I cannot.

AIKO: *(A pause then:)* Will you always be in the mirror?

THE GRAND MISTRESS OF MATSUYAMA: All your life

you will look in the mirror and be reminded of your mother.

AIKO: *(Sadly:)* But it will not really be my mother, will it?

THE GRAND MISTRESS OF MATSUYAMA: It will be you. And it will be your mother in you. It will be what she was and what you both can be in another time.

AIKO: Dolls are so lucky.

THE GRAND MISTRESS OF MATSUYAMA: Are they? They shall never breathe, never make a memory that allows them to live forever. You can breathe, Aiko-chan. Breathe. For you are more than a flower: you are a woman.

(Aiko takes a deep breath and steps toward the scrim. The Kokeshi frown sadly.)

KOKESHI: Oh no never never no!

FIRST KOKESHI: Do not leave us!

SECOND KOKESHI: Do not go away to the growing up place!

THIRD KOKESHI: They will change you, rearrange you!

AIKO: I think it is time for dinner.

KOKESHI: *(A friendly warning:)* But the stomach war! The stomach war! Trampling horses! Typhoon! Monsoon! Tornadoes in the water!

AIKO: Silly kokeshi. Sweet things.

FIRST KOKESHI: It will hurt so much to grow up!

SECOND KOKESHI: Do not let your aunt burn us up in the fire!

AIKO: I shall protect you with my dying breath.

THIRD KOKESHI: Do not forget about us!

AIKO: Do not forget about me when I am no longer a little girl. *(Bowing to The Grand Mistress of Matsuyama:)* Sayoonara. Thank you.

THE GRAND MISTRESS OF MATSUYAMA: Endure, persevere, ne, Aiko-chan.

KOKESHI: Carry on! Do not marry! Do not tarry! Aiko the adventuress! Reach for the good life not the would life!

AIKO: You really should rest, dear dolls.

KOKESHI: Oh no! We cannot sleep! Too much fun to reap! We will think of you and try not to be blue! Poor you! No rest! Life is nothing but a test!

AIKO: Goodbye!

KOKESHI: Let us play, let us play, let us play!

(Aiko steps through the scrim and the mirror world vanishes. Shakuhachi music fades in. Aiko grows weak and loses her balance. The Kuro-ko aids her. She falls and crawls toward the red kimono and crimson petals. Music ceases. With determination Aiko pulls herself to standing, politely refusing the help of the Kuro-ko who bows to her honorably. As Aiko exits, the Kuro-ko assumes the waki position. Lights crossfade...)

SCENE 6: HOMECOMING OF AGE

(Lights fade up on Aiko's home. Otoosan and Yukiko Obasan kneel at a low table eating a meal. Yukiko Obasan eats ravenously. She is visibly with child. She is exhausted and her attitude is considerably more humble. Aiko enters.)

AIKO: Otoosan?

(Otoosan drops his food in shock. Yukiko Obasan faints.)

OTOOSAN: Anta. Aiko!

AIKO: Hello, Father.

OTOOSAN: Aiko...

AIKO: Is she all right?

OTOOSAN: *(Not looking in Yukiko Obasan's direction:)* Yes, yes. *(Then looks at her and immediately holds her in his arms and fans her.)*

No, I mean —

(Stops and looks at Aiko with incredulity.)

I...I thought you were dead.

AIKO: I am very alive. Did you look for me all night?

OTOOSAN: All night? Aiko-chan, you have been gone for two winters!

AIKO: Two winters? *(Staring at Yukiko Obasan's stomach:)* I see.

OTOOSAN: That night, I saw your kimono in the snow. I had given you up for dead, but we could not find your body. Your aunt looked for you tirelessly. Where have you been?

(Yukiko Obasan moans.)

Anta. Wake up, wake up.

AIKO: She felt it important to find me? But she is with child now.

OTOOSAN: Yes. We think it is a girl, another little girl.

AIKO: A new little girl for you, for this house.

OTOOSAN: She cried for you, Aiko-chan.

AIKO: For me?

OTOOSAN: Yes. She felt that she had failed you.

(Aiko stares at her father's hand, which clasps her aunt's hand tightly. Aiko unwraps her furoshiki to reveal the red petals and materials. Otoosan is shocked.)

Has someone hurt you?

AIKO: No. I am...changing. I am becoming a woman.

(Otoosan does not comprehend at first. Yukiko Obasan sputters awake and stares wide-eyed at Aiko. She kowtows to Aiko.)

YUKIKO OBASAN: You are a ghost returned from the dead! What can I offer you, most honorable spirit?

(Aiko touches her aunt's hand with affection, but Yukiko Obasan jumps.)

AIKO: I am sorry, dear aunt.

YUKIKO OBASAN: Honorable Spirit, may I feed you fruit and tea?

AIKO: It is Aiko, just Aiko. Touch me, Aunt.

YUKIKO OBASAN: No, no.

OTOOSAN: It is all right. She has returned. She was lost.

YUKIKO OBASAN: Aiko? Is it truly you?

AIKO: Yes, Obasan.

YUKIKO OBASAN: I was afraid you died out in the cold, all because I wanted to destroy your dolls. What has happened to you? Have you been hurt?

AIKO: I have become a woman, Obasan.

YUKIKO OBASAN: My dear child, dear young woman.

(Aiko sits beside her aunt.)

AIKO: Will it always hurt?

YUKIKO OBASAN: Maybe, maybe not. It is a clean pain. It is a river of life. Feel? Did you feel her kick?

AIKO: Now you must have these.

(Gives her the furoshiki.)

You may take my dolls now.

YUKIKO OBASAN: No. Please keep them.

AIKO: Are you sure?

YUKIKO OBASAN: They are a part of you, and of your mother.

AIKO: If you truly do not mind, I would like to keep them. Maybe you will allow your new child to be my little sister and I will hand these down to her.

YUKIKO OBASAN: How kind of you.

AIKO: As for you Father, you must no longer be silent.

OTOOSAN: Aiko!

AIKO: You must tell us your secrets.

OTOOSAN: It is not the custom.

AIKO: But I need to hear you, Otoosan.

YUKIKO OBASAN: He will be with me when the child is born.

AIKO: Is that true?

OTOOSAN: *(Embarrassed:)* I have asked for permission.

AIKO: My little sister...she will need to have beautiful dolls to play with. And when she becomes a young woman, I will hold her in my arms and sing songs to her.

YUKIKO OBASAN: We will polish the dolls and keep them in view, for memories must live. Is that not so, Otoosan?

OTOOSAN: I—well— *(A pause then:)* I...I see your mother in your face.

(Aiko takes out the mirror and stares into it. She hears the wind chimes and laughter. It makes her smile. It is almost as if Otoosan and Yukiko Obasan hear it as well. They look around the room and then try to deny with their expression that

anything is out of sorts.)

AIKO: This mirror can reflect the whole world. And, after all, that is what we see when we look at other people, at flowers, at the mountains. Reflections of the light.

> *(While speaking, Aiko moves down stage. The scrim lights up; we see The Grand Mistress of Matsuyama and Kokeshi at play. Tooriko enters carrying a baby in bunting. Aiko looks around in wonder.)*

Ah...think of all the new little girls...!

> *(As lights fade out, the Kokeshi sing "Haru Ga Kita":)*

KOKESHI: HARU GA KITA

HARU GA KITA

DOKO NI KITA

YAMA NI KITA

SATO NI KITA

NO NI MO KITA*

> *(End of play.)*

28 Spring Has Come
春が来た

Words by Tatsuyuki Takano
Music by Teiichi Okano

* "*Spring is coming/ Spring is coming/ Where is it coming?/ Here in the mountains/ Here in the village/ And here in the fields./ Flowers are blooming/ Flowers are blooming/ Where are flowers blooming?/ Here in the mountains/ Here in the village/ And here in the fields.*"

The Author Speaks

What inspired you to write this play?
I was inspired to write the play because I wanted to explore the struggle that a young woman faces in the process of growing up without her mother. Because I grew up in a transnational household that was a mélange of several cultures, particularly Japanese culture, which included folklore that ignored the boundary between the natural and supernatural worlds, I was interested in placing my protagonist in a world where the lines between reality and a magical world were blurred. Along with that, I wanted the protagonist to struggle with notions of what is real and what is magical in life. During her journey, she learns a great deal about the meaning of life and it helps her to grow.

Was the structure or other elements of the play influenced by any other work?
The magical realism of the play is influenced by the traditional Japanese folklore that was inherent in the stories that my Japanese mother shared with me when I was growing up. The protagonist's dolls that come to life are drawn from the Japanese kokeshi dolls that my mother had and that I have today. I also remember my mother telling me that she tossed her dolls into the river when her mother died. To her, her mother's death signaled the end of her childhood. The protagonist in my play is very much in the same place. Finally, there is a very old Japanese fairy tale that has the same title as the play. It inspired me, but I didn't want to adapt it. My mother comes from Matsuyama, so that was a driving force in setting a play in that city.

Have you dealt with the same theme in other works that you have written?
In many of my plays, central relationships are between

mothers and daughters or between sisters. This play shares that centrality in that three of the key relationships of the protagonist are with her mother/her mother's spirit, her older sister, and her aunt/stepmother. Included in these views is the theme of coming of age. This theme also is present in other plays of mine, both TYA and non-TYA. For example, my play *Hula Heart*, a TYA play, focuses on a young male protagonist who comes of age when his family moves from Hawaii to Southern California.

What writers have had the most profound effect on your style?
I cannot say that any particular writer has had an effect on my style. My interest in the works of other writers—playwrights, poets, novelists, and essays—is quite broad and eclectic. One thing that is rather constant in my style is what has often been termed Japanese magical realism. I am quite certain that emanates from the Japanese legends, fairy tales, and folk tales that my mother shared with me when I was growing up.

What do you hope to achieve with this work?
I hope that *The Matsuyama Mirror* will gain interest from non-Asian-American arenas as well as Asian-American. I feel that its themes apply universally to many cultures as young people, particularly girls, struggle with the challenges of growing up, including the critical challenges of puberty. I think it is a play that would do well in schools and educational theatre, but I also think that its themes can reach beyond that to make a mark on an even broader audience.

What were the biggest challenges involved in the writing of this play?
The biggest challenge involved in the writing of this play was to create an aesthetically pleasing way to present a young girl's passage into puberty. I chose to use the art of dance as

well as textiles as theatrical devices. I ask not only for dance, but the use of red silk to convey the young girl's passage. Furthermore, I was confronted with how to make dolls come to life. I created a stylized way for them to speak, a type of dialogue that heightened their consciousness, thus hopefully lending it some charm and enchantment above and beyond everyday speech.

What are the most common mistakes that occur in productions of your work?
The most common error that I find in productions of my work is that the humor inherent to all drama is lost or perhaps never even discerned. I feel that all drama must include humor. In our deepest, darkest moments, lightness must slip in and jar the soul, perhaps even causing us to feel a little bit embarrassed. But, nonetheless, we are tickled, even if for a moment. Finding these moments of lightness gives drama the balance that it needs to be human.

What inspired you to become a playwright?
When I was five years old, I told my Japanese mother that one day she would see my name on a book. She smiled and said that Japanese immigrants could not become artists; it would have to wait a generation. Why I wanted to be a writer, I don't know. There were no writers in my family. There were no published voices that, at that age, had profoundly affected me. In the small town in which I lived, there was not even a legitimate theatre where I might have seen plays. But I felt in my bones that writing for the stage was my calling and I followed it.

Are any characters modeled after real life or historical figures?
The character of Aiko, the protagonist, is modeled after a real-life figure (that of my mother).

Shakespeare gave advice to the players in *Hamlet*; if you could give advice to your cast what would it be?
If I could give advice to a cast for *The Matsuyama Mirror*, I would encourage them to find the balance of the drama with the humor. I also would encourage them to go openly and courageously into the aesthetics of the play. I would suggest the same for the magical realism.

About the Author

Internationally produced playwright **Velina Hasu Houston** is the recipient of 21 commissions from institutions such as The Pasadena Playhouse, Mark Taper Forum, Los Angeles Opera, Silk Road/Goodman Theatre, Manhattan Theatre Club, Playwrights' Arena, and others; some of her producers include these theatres along with Pittsburgh Public Theatre, Old Globe Theatre, and TheatreWorks. In addition to YouthPLAYS, publishers include Dramatists Play Service, Smith and Kraus, Vintage Books/Random House, *Los Angeles Times, American Theatre, The Dramatist,* and others. She has written for Columbia Pictures, PBS, and several indies; and co-produced *Desert Dreamers* (Peter Fonda, narrator). Honors include the Kennedy Center, Rockefeller Foundation, Japan Foundation, Lila Wallace-Readers' Digest Foundation, American Film Institute, Pinter Review Prize for Drama, and others. At the USC School of Dramatic Arts, she is creator/director of the Master of Fine Arts in Dramatic Writing. She served on the Department of State's Japan-US Friendship Commission and conducted her Fulbright Scholar project at Aoyama Gakuin Daigaku, Tokyo. http://www.velinahasuhouston.com

About YouthPLAYS

YouthPLAYS (www.youthplays.com) is a publisher of award-winning professional dramatists and talented new discoveries, each with an original theatrical voice, and all dedicated to expanding the vocabulary of theatre for young actors and audiences. On our website you'll find one-act and full-length plays and musicals for teen and pre-teen (and even college) actors, as well as duets and monologues for competition. Many of our authors' works have been widely produced at high schools and middle schools, youth theatres and other TYA companies, both amateur and professional, as well as at elementary schools, camps, churches and other institutions serving young audiences and/or actors worldwide. Most are intended for performance by young people, while some are intended for adult actors performing for young audiences.

YouthPLAYS was co-founded by professional playwrights Jonathan Dorf and Ed Shockley. It began merely as an additional outlet to market their own works, which included a substantial body of award-winning published and unpublished plays and musicals. Those interested in their published plays were directed to the respective publishers' websites, and unpublished plays were made available in electronic form. But when they saw the desperate need for material for young actors and audiences—coupled with their experience that numerous quality plays for young people weren't finding a home—they made the decision to represent the work of other playwrights as well. Dozens and dozens of authors are now members of the YouthPLAYS family, with scripts available both electronically and in traditional acting editions. We continue to grow as we look for exciting and challenging plays and musicals for young actors and audiences.

About ProduceaPlay.com

Let's put up a play! Great idea! But producing a play takes time, energy and knowledge. While finding the necessary time and energy is up to you, ProduceaPlay.com is a website designed to assist you with that third element: knowledge.

Created by YouthPLAYS' co-founders, Jonathan Dorf and Ed Shockley, ProduceaPlay.com serves as a resource for producers at all levels as it addresses the many facets of production. As Dorf and Shockley speak from their years of experience (as playwrights, producers, directors and more), they are joined by a group of award-winning theatre professionals and experienced teachers from the world of academic theatre, all making their expertise available for free in the hope of helping this and future generations of producers, whether it's at the school or university level, or in community or professional theatres.

The site is organized into a series of major topics, each of which has its own page that delves into the subject in detail, offering suggestions and links for further information. For example, Publicity covers everything from Publicizing Auditions to How to Use Social Media to Posters to whether it's worth hiring a publicist. Casting details Where to Find the Actors, How to Evaluate a Resume, Callbacks and even Dealing with Problem Actors. You'll find guidance on your Production Timeline, The Theater Space, Picking a Play, Budget, Contracts, Rehearsing the Play, The Program, House Management, Backstage, and many other important subjects.

The site is constantly under construction, so visit often for the latest insights on play producing, and let it help make your play production dreams a reality.

More from YouthPLAYS

Xtigone by Nambi E. Kelley
Drama. 90-100 minutes. 5-15+ females, 4-15+ males (9-30+ performers possible).

Chicago. Present day. Xtigone's brothers have been killed in drive-by shootings by each other's rival gang. Her powerful uncle calls for the bodies to be buried instead of uncovering the violence in the city streets. In this re-imagining of Sophocles' ***Antigone*** that uses poetry, dance and dialogue that speak with an urban voice, will Xtigone go against his edict and risk death in her quest for her community's truth?

HKFN: The Abbreviated Adventures of Huckleberry Finn by Jeff Goode
Comedy. 25-35 minutes. 3-8 females, 2-6 males (5-10 performers possible).

The actor playing Huck runs away from a production of Twain's controversial classic, ***The Adventures of Huckleberry Finn***. But when the actor who plays Jim runs away too and troublemakers Duke & King join in, their fugitive theatre company launches into a series of misadventures—while the domineering Aunt Polly tries to force them back into the "real" play. In the chaos, that play—and its discussion about race—may be happening without them knowing it.

The Locker Next 2 Mine by Jonathan Dorf
Dramedy. 80-85 minutes. 5-12+ males, 8-16+ females (14-40 performers possible).

Alisa arrives at a new high school in the middle of the year to find her locker next to a shrine for a popular lacrosse player who's died in an auto accident, but as she digs deeper, she discovers another death that no one talks about, even as it's left many of the students trying to pick up their own pieces. A play about teen suicide and dealing with loss.

Blood, Sweat, and Cheers by Kaci Beeler and Amy Gentry
Comedy. 85-100 minutes. 7-20 females, 3-6 males (15-30 performers possible).

Seventeen-year-old June returns to her old cheer gym, the notoriously competitive Austin Cheer Depot, after an abrupt two-year sabbatical. While some of her old teammates are glad she's back, rival and cheer captain Kennedy is not pleased. June battles her teammates, her parents, her coaches, her best friend James and herself to make it to the top...but is being the best worth losing everything?

The Exceptional Childhood Center by Dylan Schifrin
Comedy. 25-35 minutes. 2-4 females, 2-3 males (5-6 performers possible).

Reggie Watson has been accepted into the right preschool. He's set for life...as long as he can make it through the one-day trial period. But when desperation breeds disaster and his future hangs in the balance, Reggie and his band of quirky classmates may just discover things about themselves that school could never teach them.

Jennifer the Unspecial: Time Travel, Love Potions & 8th Grade by Matthew Mezzacappa (book & lyrics) & Cynthia Chi-Wing Wong (music)
Musical. 90 minutes. 5-30 males, 3-30 females (8-60 performers possible).

When her science teacher's invention goes horribly wrong, awkward, clumsy eighth grader Jennifer finds herself thrust into a time-traveling adventure with three of her classmates. Through the journey, as they encounter warriors, artists, presidents and love potions, Jennifer discovers she doesn't need anyone's approval to be absolutely amazing and special.

And We Will Share the Sky by Donna Latham

Dramedy. 50-60 minutes. 3-5+ females, 3-4+ males (6-8+ performers possible).

Our story takes place long ago, when Brother Sun and Sister Moon still lived on land. They love each other dearly, but the siblings just can't live together. They are as different as, well, as day and night. Gadabout Sun shines a dazzling personality over endless friends. Contemplative Moon, an artist, finds inspiration within. The two struggle to live with their differences, until Sun's love for his watery new friend Marina changes everything in this play for young audiences inspired by traditional tales of Nigeria and Senegal.

The Boston Massacre by Ed Shockley

Drama. 40-50 minutes. Flexible cast of 14-50.

A modern painter struggles to capture the essence of the King Street Custom House clash immortalized in the engravings of Paul Revere. The entire stage is a canvas, and actors create tableaux with their bodies, exploring the deadly confrontation between soldiers and townsmen from every imaginable perspective as they arrive at a final portrait that communicates the immortal themes that inspired a new nation.

The Ghost Moments by Randy Wyatt

Drama. 45-70 minutes. 1-10 females, 1-5 males (2-15 performers total).

We all have ghosts that haunt us. Some are literal: Matty tries to rid his sister's apartment of a spirit that may or may not be there, Zachary prepares his bunker for the zombie apocalypse. Others are metaphorical: Marianne's absent father, Caroline's memories of water, Carver's secret powers. As we witness hauntings and exorcisms through a series of monologues, this group of characters and their loves, longings, joy and pain, will haunt us long after the curtain falls.

Made in the USA
Columbia, SC
02 August 2020